JAMIE ARMITAGE

An Interrogation, Jamie Armitage's first play, opened at Summerhall, Edinburgh in August 2023, where it enjoyed an award-winning, sold-out run, before transferring to Hampstead Theatre, London.

Jamie is co-director of *SIX: The Musical*, which is currently playing in the West End, on Broadway, and multiple other locations worldwide. For his work on *SIX* he was nominated for a Tony Award for Best Direction of a Musical.

Other directing credits include *The Red and the Black* (Tokyo Metropolitan Theatre); *Straight Line Crazy* (The Shed; co-directed with Nicholas Hytner); *Southern Belles: A Tennessee Williams Double Bill* (King's Head Theatre); *Spring Awakening* and *Sweeney Todd* (RCSSD); *And Tell Sad Stories of the Death of Queens* (King's Head Theatre); *Love Me Now* (Tristan Bates Theatre).

He is an Associate Director of the Bridge Theatre. He was a resident director at the Almeida Theatre from 2019 to 2021, and an associate artist at the King's Head Theatre.

Jamie Armitage

A GHOST IN YOUR EAR

NICK HERN BOOKS

London

www.nickhernbooks.co.uk

A Nick Hern Book

A Ghost In Your Ear first published in Great Britain in 2025 as a paperback original by Nick Hern Books Limited, The Glasshouse, 49a Goldhawk Road, London W12 8QP

Cover image: Rebecca Pitt

Designed and typeset by Nick Hern Books, London
Printed in the UK by Mimeo Ltd, Huntingdon, Cambridgeshire PE29 6XX

A CIP catalogue record for this book is available from the British Library

ISBN 978 1 83904 511 0

www.nickhernbooks.co.uk/environmental-policy

Nick Hern Books' authorised representative in the EU is
Easy Access System Europe – Mustamäe tee 50, 10621 Tallinn, Estonia
email gpsr.requests@easproject.com

To Dad

(for not being like this)

Thanks

To everyone who read and helped to craft this play: Ruby Thomas, Jack Bradfield, Talia Burrows-Ward, Dylan Pager, Sophieclaire Armitage, Howard Carter, Letty Thomas, Ellie Keel, Hannah Farley-Hills, Gurnesha Bola and the legendary Mel Kenyon.

And of course, my collaborators Ben & Max Ringham.

J.A.

A Ghost In Your Ear was first performed at Hampstead Theatre, London, on 6 December 2025, produced by Hannah Farley-Hills for HFH Productions. The cast was as follows:

GEORGE	George Blagden
SID	Jonathan Livingstone

Writer and Director	Jamie Armitage
Sound Designer	Ben and Max Ringham
Set and Costume Designer	Anisha Fields
Lighting Designer	Ben Jacobs
Dramaturg	Gurnesha Bola
Casting Director	Becky Paris CDG
Movement Consultant	Robert Strange

Characters

GEORGE, *an actor. Late twenties to mid-thirties. The name of
the character should change to match the performer playing
the role*
SID, *a sound technician. Mid-thirties*

The Audience

Every audience member will have headphones. These are linked
to a binaural microphone shaped like a human head which will
be on-stage during the show. There will also be a number of
pre-recorded sound-effects.

Sounds

Sound effects are written in like this:

Tap.   **Tap.**   **Tap.**

These can be heard by the audience in their headphones. I've
only written in ones which are narratively crucial. There are
other sounds described (snow crunching under foot, creaking
staircases, etc.) which would be audible as well, yet are more
for atmospheric purposes.

Essentially, if the text mentions a sound, the audience will hear it.

*This text went to press before the end of rehearsals and so may
differ slightly from the play as performed.*

As the audience enter the auditorium, there are headphones attached to their seats.

The set itself is invisible behind a glass wall, so the audience can only see their own terrified reflections.

As they take their seats, a pre-recorded message is playing in their headphones.

A VOICE *in the headphones. An unsettling soft tone. Not much more than a whisper. Imagine Christopher Lee or Mark Gatiss speaking softly into your ear:*

VOICE Welcome.

We want you to feel as comfortable as possible.

You should now hear a voice in your left ear.

Voice is only in left headphone.

You should now hear a voice in your right ear.

Voice in right headphone.

Left ear.

Voice in left.

Right ear.

Voice in right.

If you experience any problems, please raise your hand and someone will help you.

Take a moment to turn off your phone. Yes, *off*. The signal interferes with the technology.

If everything is working as it should be, then relax – if you can... the show will begin shortly.

Eventually –

Show begins.

Darkness.

Good. So, you've made it this far.

What you are about to watch is a horror story. If you choose to leave, you will not be allowed back in. You have been warned.

We recommend you wear your headphones throughout, but especially whenever the red recording light is turned on.

The red recording light flashes.

If at any moment, you are too scared, simply remove your headphones and the voices will disappear.

Remember the ghost is not real, it is only in your ear...

A rumble builds.

Then –

A recording studio appears.

In the centre, a large grey, binaural microphone in the shape of a human head. Through a glass window at the back, we see a control booth with a mixing desk.

The walls are covered in sound-absorbent dark-grey foam which gives the whole space a spiky, oppressive atmosphere.

GEORGE *appears through the doorway. Peering around.*

GEORGE   Hello? Anybody here?

Pokes his head into the studio.

Sid?

SID   (*off-stage, over the speaker*) One evening a lost man wanders into a recording studio. He's late. Very late.

GEORGE   I know, I know.

SID   A bold move when the recording is due tomorrow.

GEORGE   Yeah, but –

SID   The poor sound engineer will have to work through the night to get the mix done in time.

GEORGE   I'm sorry, sorry.

SID   His words mean nothing. How will George pay for his grievous sin?

GEORGE   Peanut-butter protein balls and a pack of Camel Blues?

SID   (*gasp*) This is an expectant father you're talking to.

GEORGE   Two packs?

SID   Done.

SID *appears at the booth window, then enters through the door.*

GEORGE   Enjoying your new den?

SID   Bro, you won't even – they splurged big. Like it's not fully done. Needs more paint out there, and I swear bits have only been blu-tacked in place. But kit-wise we are set. Best I ever had.

GEORGE	So worth trekking out to the world's saddest retail park?
SID	Oooh, sorry it's not the Soho-convenience you're used to.
GEORGE	At least there are other people in Soho.
SID	Quiet is good. And they'll finish the other units eventually. You'll get your Gail's, but for the mo it's just us two…
GEORGE	Lucky us two. And that's the –

They both look at the binaural microphone.

SID	The head. The dome microphone. It'll pick you up wherever you are and then puts your voice into the same position when someone listens to it with their headphones

GEORGE *approaches the expressionless head with reverence.*

We'll get the script up there own those screens, so feel free to move around and – wait, put these on.

SID *grabs a pair of headphones.*

GEORGE	Okay.
SID	Close your eyes. Can you hear the room? Its tone.
GEORGE	Uh-huh.
SID	I'm gonna move around the head. Hear that?
GEORGE	Yep, yep.
SID	I'm getting further away.

SID *scurries to the booth excitedly. And plays a sound.*

GEORGE   …is that you…?

SID   Nope!!

The pair are very buzzed about this.

And I've got these pre-records that I'll mix into the finished thing like… standard-standard: creaky door.

door creaks

Gusty wind.

wind howling

But then this is where it gets cool with the positioning stuff.

Someone walking behind you.

sound of footsteps walking behind you

He's getting closer.

footsteps get nearer

He's running to catch you.

footsteps intensify

He's stopped. Where'd he go?

Oh, actually, where'd you go?

busy street sounds

Baby boy's back in Soho.

GEORGE   I got to admit that's fun.

SID   (*re-entering*) So I'll play a few simple sounds for you when we're recording just to set the moooood.

GEORGE   Do what you gotta do, Sid. And levels-wise?

SID	Just like you were speaking to somebody who was right there. It's super-sensitive. It'll pick up every cough and sniff.
GEORGE	No coughing, check. So –
SID	(*suddenly serious*) Um. Aren't you forgetting…?

GEORGE *fishes out of his jacket pocket a protein ball and a pack of cigarettes.* SID *looks down at the offering.*

GEORGE	Second pack to follow.
SID	(*snatching the offering*) Tell Sasha and I'll make your voice sound like a toad on helium.
GEORGE	How's she doing?
SID	Hippo feet and like she's swallowed a space hopper.
GEORGE	Cute.
SID	Her words, not mine.
GEORGE	When's she due?
SID	Anytime now.
GEORGE	Working up to the wire?
SID	Need to get as much done before the little dude arrives.
GEORGE	A boy? Congrats.
SID	Thanks. Sometimes I look at her and I'm like in you is half a little me – and it spins me out. But… I already know I'd do anything for him.
GEORGE	Can't wait to be the godfather.
SID	When have we ever seen each other outside of one of these booths?

GEORGE	Oh, I was –
SID	Ahh, just razzing you. Plus, I thought you didn't want them?
GEORGE	Never say never, but in truth – nah. Also, saying I don't want them is my go-to excuse for escaping romantic entanglements...
SID	Could be good for you...
GEORGE	Sure, but if it's not, then it's a bit late to discover that once it's born.
SID	Every guy worries about that though. I did.
GEORGE	It's just, like, uh –
SID	Let it out, George. Your secrets have and will always be safe in Sid's confession booth.
GEORGE	I know this sounds – but I don't want the responsibility. I enjoy providing for myself and doing what I want, when I want. With no – burdens.
SID	Yeah, it's not the same awesome, but like a different kind of awesome. It transformed my brother entirely. He never thought he knew how to be cos of how we grew up without ours – then (*exhales forcefully*) perfect dad.
GEORGE	Sure, I get it's great for some people, but just not me.
SID	Why?
GEORGE	I'm very driven.
SID	Cheers.
GEORGE	Not that you're not, but like, I've spent so much energy trying to not turn into

	my dad, that if I can't give the time to be a great one, then why bother?
SID	Fair play.
GEORGE	What's with all the prying?
SID	Just – checking. If you're gonna be a godfather I wanna make sure you won't yeet my boy out the window first chance ya get.
GEORGE	I don't like, hate them. They're just not for me. Career comes first.
SID	Drowning in work then?
GEORGE	Not at the – but it'll pick up. Thanks for this gig by the way. I know you put in a good word –
SID	It's chill.
GEORGE	But still. It's been a bit quiet recently, and you've no idea how much I needed this.
SID	I kinda did.
GEORGE	Ha, thank you. So, what we doing? My agent didn't send through a script or much –
SID	Just the fee?
GEORGE	Well, yeah.
SID	No shade, no shame. This is proper money. Makes Audible cheques look like sofa change.
GEORGE	Who's it for?
SID	Like a proof of concept for some kind of new horror start-up. They wanna know if there's a future in binaural ghost stories. Essentially, they're rich and love the sound of your voice almost as much as you do.

GEORGE   Flattered.

SID   Words will be up be on the screen there.
            And they want to hear your real fear.

GEORGE   What does that mean?

SID   Pretend to be scared and get paid?

GEORGE   I think I can just about manage that.

SID   Do some of your 'look at me, I went to
            clown school' stuff. But stick to a single
            take as much as poss.

GEORGE   One-take wonder it is. Do we need to
            wild track anything first or –

SID   Nah, might grab some gasps, screams,
            standard scare package at the end, but
            otherwise –

GEORGE   Straight in?

SID   Straight on in.

            SID *heads back in to the booth, while*
            GEORGE *does some vibey vocal warm-
            ups.*

            (*visible at the control desk*) When you're
            finished with your cat singing, we can –

            GEORGE *gives* SID *a thumbs up.*

            Then, that's us good to go. And we…
            are… Recording.

            Red recording light switches on.

            GEORGE *steadies himself, he's
            transformed, primed, ready to –*

            An odd electronic sound

            Wait, wait. I'm getting some interference.

GEORGE   What?

SID	Have you got your phone on?
GEORGE	Oh yeah, sorry. I'll turn it –
SID	Better leave it out here. That mic's hypersensitive.
GEORGE	Oh, sure. I'll just –
	GEORGE *goes to the door and pulls at it. It's locked.*
	Sid, the door?
SID	Ah, sound proofing – it seals when we're live.
	Turns off recording light. The door opens.
GEORGE	Thank you.
	GEORGE *gives* SID *his phone and reenters.*
	Okay, now I'm ready to –
SID	Roll? Rock?
GEORGE	Record.
SID	Near enough. Take it away.
GEORGE	*(reading, in different voices, trying to find his groove)* 'A Ghost In Your Ear *by A.C. Pritchitt.' 'A Ghost In Your Ear *by A.C. Pritchitt.' 'A Ghost In Your Ear *by A.C. Pritchitt.'*
SID	Pick a voice, any voice.
	GEORGE *swears at* SID *over his shoulder, clears his throat and begins.*
GEORGE	'A Ghost In Your Ear *by A.C. Pritchitt.'*

For a man as mean-spirited as my father, dying in January made perfect sense. When every day is short and grey, his sudden death was a final bleak flourish to an always bleak month. His lawyer called with the news. I was horizontal on my sofa, wallowing in post-breakup self-pity, when his name lit up my phone screen. It wasn't her name though – who I'd been hoping, who I'd been wanting to call me – yet still after a moment I answered. He gave me his condolences on the death of my father; I said that was unnecessary. He asked if I would be attending the funeral; I told him I would not. He checked if there was anything else he could do for me; I replied that there wasn't. Then he paused for a moment as if I might say something; I didn't, so he assured me that everything would be settled swiftly, before hanging up.

Now, I don't want you to think I'm unfeeling in the reaction to my father's death but when you haven't seen someone in twenty-three years, death is really just the continuation of an absence. Nothing more. I only saw him once or twice after he abandoned me and my mother when I was three years old, and disappeared to his old family home. My mum was as steady as she could be and barely mentioned him, except on certain nights when she had a drink or two too many, and all her confusion and hurt over being deserted came pouring out. I think this pain plagued her until the end. I was with her when her life support was switched off, so I know what it is to be there for a parent. But with him, my father, I didn't want any part of it.

The day the second call came, I was at a loose end but pretending to be positive. True, my dad had just died, and I'd been let go from my university post after missing out on tenure, again. And yes, there'd also been the breakup because despite how committed I was to her, she couldn't understand that I wasn't ready for all the things she wanted, like marriage, wallpaper, and children.

GEORGE   My kind of guy.

SID looks annoyed and signals to keep going.

Sorry, sorry…

She said having a child would open a chamber in my heart I didn't know existed. I told her that it's quite hard to stuff a baby back in a chamber if it turned out I didn't want it. She didn't find that funny...

I was gazing absentmindedly out the window on a Wednesday morning when my phone rang. I snatched it up, but it still wasn't her, and two weeks after his first call I heard the blocked-nose voice of the lawyer again.

'Sorry to disturb you. I'm sure you must be very busy.' I stopped fiddling with the curtain toggle and fixed my face in a more business-like expression. 'An issue has arisen with settling your father's wishes, specifically his desire for his house to be cleared by a removal team prior to its being demolished.'

I frowned, yet Mr Morrison just ploughed on.

'The company your father received the original quote from, no longer wants the job. I have found a similar removal team yet their fee is significantly higher, by a margin of five thousand pounds. I need your permission to authorise this payment and allow the clearing of the house to begin.'

I said nothing for a moment. One of his dry coughs. Then –

'Of course, I could keep looking but this is the lowest I have so far from a local firm that would be – willing to take the job.'

I stared out the window. It looked like the sun had made no effort to rise. Just greyness, which stretched out beyond the crowd of buildings.

'Do I have your permission to proceed?'

I rested my head against the window. The cold glass soothed the roaring in my mind.

'I'll do it.'

'Sorry?' the lawyer replied.

'I'll come. Clear the house myself, do all the – whatever. I can do it.'

There was a pause at the other end of the phone.

'That was not your father's wish. He was very specific – '

'I know.'

'He told me himself that he didn't want to cause you any bother that – '

'That he wanted to keep me away?'

'In a manner of speaking, but – '

'I know, but he's dead isn't he?'

I understood what was behind my father's wishes: he didn't think I was capable of it. Even in death he was determined that our lives should be as separate as possible.

'I'll do it myself. I'll catch the train up tomorrow.'

'Wouldn't that be an imposition on your schedule?'

I didn't blink before lying and replying, 'I'm sure I can make some adjustments. My Head of Department will understand.'

'Well, I'll meet you at the station. Just after three then – um, yes. I'll meet you.' And with that, he was gone.

I smiled in triumph. This felt like purpose.
I pulled a suitcase down from the top of the
wardrobe, and for the first time since the
breakup wasn't bothered by the empty hangers
inside as I flung clothes into the bag. In that
moment, I felt truly excited. This is what I'd
needed – a proper task. Not a child to open
some mystical chamber in my heart.

GEORGE   Is this why you kept asking me about
            kids? A trigger warning?

SID   (*taps his watch*)

GEORGE   Sure, sure. (*continues*)

Yet if I'd known what I know now, I would have
respected my father's wishes and never gone
anywhere near that house.

* * *

During the third hour of the journey north, as
I stared out the window at the frost-covered
fields of Yorkshire, then County Durham,
I remembered the last time I'd seen my father
twenty-three years ago. It had been in a
motorway service station, a neutral ground
I suppose. My mother kept an eye from a distant
picnic table. He'd been awkward; one hand kept
rubbing his neck and he never quite looked
directly at me. Yet I was so delighted to see
him that I ran into his arms and hugged him
closely. He held me in a brittle embrace before
straightening up and saying not to lean my head
into a hug as it was 'unmanly'. I think I must have
been about nine years old at the time.

There had been the odd postcard on birthdays
and the even odder phone calls where he'd ring
and ask me to tell him 'What was what'. As soon
as I asked about his life, he always found a reason

to hang up. It didn't hurt me; it was just how it was. How he was.

As the train took me closer to where he'd hidden himself away, my curiosity to finally see the house, his house grew. After two transfers at increasingly desolate stations, I ended up on a train which wheezed along a single track through the Pennines, and deposited me on a platform in the remotest village I had ever seen in my life.

Not being able to drive is one of those traits which is cute in your twenties but feels like an assault on maturity in your thirties. As I waited, I vowed that this was the last time I would be standing, shivering at a station waiting to be picked up by anyone, least of all a morbid, little death lawyer.

When he eventually pulled up, he peered at me through his too-thick glasses as he leaned across to open the passenger door of his small, green car.

'Get in, get in,' he barked at me.

I pushed my bag onto the back seat and clambered in next to him. We drove in silence for the first twenty minutes, heading deeper and deeper into what seemed, to my London eyes, to be true wilderness.

Eventually, I piped up with, 'Don't think much of this weather?'

'The snow's coming in soon.'

'Oh, snow. How nice.' I tried to brighten the mood. 'Must make it very pretty.'

'Except when it cuts off the only road back down to town.'

Beyond the windscreen, small flurries danced through the air. The minute fuck-ulations –

GEORGE   Minute fluctcha – fuckya-ations. Mi –
nute urgh! Fuck you, AC Pritchitt, and
your minute fluctuations, you wordy
bastard. (*exhale*) I'll go again.

GEORGE *shakes it off and bounces
around, sips some water, then –*

The minute fluctuations of snow seemed
innocent enough, yet I could imagine how
this small, winding road would be completely
blocked after a blizzard. We passed empty field
after empty field, as the car wound up the narrow
path into the hills.

Our uncompanionable silence lasted until he
pulled over at the end of a long driveway. Two
cracked stone columns flanked the entrance and
I could just make out the imposing grey building
in the distance.

'Aren't we going to...' Nodding towards the
driveway. Hopefully indicating my desire to be
dropped a little nearer the house itself.

'Rain's churned up the drive. Don't want to get
stuck.'

'Right...'

'Call if you need me to bring you anything or
when you're done or – wish to leave.'

'I can always get a taxi.'

'No taxis round here.'

'Well, I could walk back down the road.'

'You could.'

'But you wouldn't?'

'Not me who'd be prising your frozen body out
of a ditch.'

'I guess I'll be staying put then.'

He continued to stare at me. It was as if his eyes were trying to tell me something that he couldn't bring himself to say. 'I got some supplies. Just to tide you over.'

He pushed a heavy carrier bag onto my lap. Generous, I guess, but also deliberately highlighting my lack of preparation. He then muttered, 'I also checked with other removal companies and found some more affordable prices – '

'I'm here now, and it'll take a few days at most.'

'Hm.' His disbelief in me flickered across his face, but then, 'You'll need this.' He handed me an envelope. 'Keys for the house. Instructions from your father.'

'Thank you.' I glanced down at the familiar blue scrawl on the yellow paper.

'And – '

I looked at the hesitating man.

'And – call me. For anything. You understand?'

Again that odd expression, almost like some judgemental little reptile. I didn't let it get to me though and just thanked him vaguely, pulled my bag from the back seat then started the long trudge up the drive. Yet as the car drove off and the silence pressed in, I realised just how alone I was up here.

Isolation was what I needed, I told myself. Re-energise my body and my mind with clearing a big house, and maybe find time to scribble a few thoughts for a new essay. The next few days seemed to be filled with a potential that I'd been craving.

The mud squelched under foot as I got closer and closer to the house. It was strange to see it after all this time. My father had never really mentioned where he'd grown up. I'd always imagined a grand sweeping building. Somewhere between a spectacular mansion and a modest castle. Yet the house in front of me was oddly diminished.

Its front was covered in ivy which had lost its lustre in the cold and just looked like cords straining to keep the house contained. The setting sun caught the windows and made them blaze like tiny fires in the inexpressive stone face of the house.

Incongruously, two enormous yellow skips had been plonked out front, which slightly ruined any pretensions of the picturesque, yet I just chose to ignore them as I approached the front door.

I tore open the thick envelope and slid the keys onto my palm. It took two tries but eventually the lock clicked and the door swung slowly open.

Unnoticed by GEORGE, *the door to the studio opens slightly by itself.*

The hall beyond was dim and still. I paused, inhaled, then stepped into the house as the door clicked shut behind me.

* * *

The studio door shuts itself. The sound makes GEORGE *turn, but everything is still.*

GEORGE   I – I –

SID   (*whispering into the headphones*) I don't know exactly…

GEORGE   (*still distracted*) I don't know exactly, um…

SID   What I was expecting…

GEORGE

I don't know exactly what I was expecting.
Maybe the den of a mad-man. A squalid hovel of
a hermit who'd cut himself off from the world.
But it really was just a plainly decorated old
house. Maybe in its past it had been a vibrant
hub of energy. I stared at the grand staircase in
the middle of the hallway and could imagine
petticoated women flirting behind their fans
with red-jacketed soldiers as they leaned against
the beautifully carved mahogany bannisters. Yet
now the staircase was bare.

Looking around the murky hallway, it took me a
moment to realise that every window had thick
heavy curtains drawn across them. As I walked
around the hallway, I pulled back the fabric to let
in the last of the daylight. Perhaps who ever had
visited after his death had closed the curtains, yet
I reconsidered this, when I saw that huge lengths
of cloth had been thrown over every mirror too.
Perhaps my father's vanity couldn't bear the look
of his ageing face – a wrinkled reminder of all
the pain he'd caused in the world. This thought
gave me great pleasure as I freed each mirror
from its shroud.

My exploration of the ground floor eventually
led me to the kitchen which was surprisingly
simple. Each time I opened a cupboard door
I half thought there'd be the bones of a rat or
some forgotten creature. But instead there were
just orderly lines of tinned soup.

I paused when I looked at the kitchen table.
There was a place set for one, with an unused
knife and a half-filled water glass on a coaster
from his last meal. A food stained napkin was
folded neatly and placed on the back of the chair.
I picked up the napkin and imagined the old
man wiping his lips as he ate another meal alone,

as he'd done the previous night, the previous month and for many years before. I almost felt sorry for him in that moment.

I quickly dropped the napkin and headed out the other door and into a sort of parlour. In one corner was a hefty desk. I checked through the drawers which were packed with papers. It was going to be a mammoth task sifting through all that. But, a problem for tomorrow. I looked out of the glass doors which led to an overgrown lawn that sloped down to dense cluster of wild-looking trees with their bare branches waving forlornly in the wind.

One of the mic booms on the wall behind GEORGE, shifts slightly by itself. He senses the movement, but turns too slowly to see it. He shivers uneasily, and continues.

Beyond the staircase was the final room I had to explore. The door opened with a wrenching sound, to reveal a library. But not just any library, a true picture-book library. I grinned with pure joy at the leather armchair with the worn seat by the fireplace and the walls and walls of books. I walked along the shelves, brushing my finger gently over the gold-leafed titles, savouring the feel of each subtle ornate indentation. Above were thick wooden beams, each must have been the width of my torso, On the centre one, halfway along was a score mark where the wood was worn away, as if something had once hung from it – a chandelier, maybe? – yet it was impossible to tell.

The only wall which was not covered in bookshelves was obscured by a vast dust sheet. I pulled down the fabric to reveal an enormous mirror – ten-feet wide and stretching from the floor to the beams above. Yet its scale wasn't the only thing which surprised me. It was cracked – fissures erupted from a single point as though it had been struck in a fit of fury. Yet the glass had stayed in place, creating a surface with splinters here and there that looked like jagged ripples stretching out to the edges and towards me.

A soft, almost imperceptible breath on the back of the neck.

GEORGE *turns. The lights in the booth have darkened, so* GEORGE *only sees his own reflection in the glass.*

A sound of growing isolation.

The light in the booth returns, then SID *waves to get his attention, and* GEORGE *eventually continues.*

I turned and saw my father's chair by the fireplace directly in line with the broken mirror. I could imagine him in a drunken rage of self-loathing as he hurled a whisky tumbler at his reflection.

Despite this, the library had won my heart, and I could imagine myself passing many happy evenings in here. I sank back into the warm, leathery embrace of the chair. Tucked behind it was a curious wooden stool with a winch for adjusting the height. I pulled it round in front of me and fiddled with the handle. I smiled at its arthritic creaks as I ratcheted it down to a comfortable height for resting my feet. Perfectly content, I took the paper from the yellow envelope in my pocket, and began to read.

The instructions were very plain and practical: 'Please throw everything in the skips. There is nothing of value here, but if you do find anything to your taste, keep it. With the exception of items in the library. Everything in there must be incinerated.' I looked up as if to see why this room had been chosen for a special level of destruction...

I'd started to skim by the final page with its detailed explanation of different fuse boxes when the last line caught my eye. 'When you are done, tell Mr Morrison to go to the space in the blue corridor. He'll know what you mean.' The blue corridor? I hadn't seen anything on this floor which matched that description.

I suddenly stood and strode towards the stairs, wanting to see where upstairs this blue corridor was. I reached the first floor landing which stretched away in both directions, with at least a dozen doors, yet was decisively an off-yellow colour. I poked my head into each of the empty rooms, until at one end, I found a bedroom which felt like the best option for me by virtue of it still actually having a mattress on the frame of the four-poster bed.

I retraced my steps, then past the top of the stairs to the other end of the corridor and found a small staircase tucked round the corner. In every way that the main staircase was impressive and grand, this one was not. It twisted back on itself, as though it had been pushed, unwanted into a corner of the house. As I walked up, each step creaked comically under foot.

The second level was cramped as though it had been squashed to compensate for the grandeur below. The rooms here were even plainer and starker, with only metal frames of single beds and grime-stained sinks in the corners. I was just wondering where my father slept, fearing it may have been the room I'd chosen for myself when

I swung open the last door to see – I suppose
the clearest way of describing it is as being like a
monk's cell: plain walls, a small window, and a
narrow bed. I approached where my father used
to sleep. I knelt down and and pressed my nose
against the pillow. It had a smell of something,
someone, but not a scent I recognised in anyway.
I inhaled again, then stood up quickly and
walked out of the room, letting the door slam
shut behind me.

Round a corner, the grey-panelled hall came to
a dead-end, yet I still hadn't found any corridor
that could be called blue. I traipsed slowly back
downstairs past the abandoned rooms, the
peeling paint and broken light fixtures trying to
think what the blue corridor could refer to, yet
another more intrusive question kept nagging at
me: why had my father locked himself away in
this depressing place for so many years?

* * *

After I'd eaten a quick dinner, however, and read
most of the evening by the fire in the library,
I was starting to grow a little fonder of this place.
London felt like a distant, swirling scream of
burdens and responsibilities as I sat here in the
peaceful quiet of an old house, watching the
flames dance in the grate.

The red recording light flickers; GEORGE
does not see.

An early night's sleep felt like a plan, then I could
begin clearing in the morning. I snapped my
book shut and headed up to bed.

As I walked up the wide central staircase,
I paused for a moment. Because, I thought...

Step.

I took another step, then another.

Step.   **Step.**

There it was again, what seemed like the sound of steps which weren't my own. I stood still and strained my ears but only heard the silence of the house. I moved up a step. Nothing. Yet still every hair on my neck was on end. I looked down the staircase to the shadows in the hall below, trying to peer through the darkness for something moving around, but there wasn't anything there. I knew I was being absurd. Yet I still hurried along the corridor to my room slightly faster than intended, and locked the door behind me.

My worries faded when I'd got the flames in the grate going. I'd never slept in a room with a fire before. I felt like some kind of Georgian squire, though Georgian squires had servants to make their beds, I thought, as I struggled with a top sheet. I was soon settled under the covers though and the orange glow flickered –

The red recording light flickers, more noticeably; GEORGE stops for a beat, then carries on.

– soothingly on the wall every time I looked up from my book. It was the most peaceful I had felt in a very, very long time. Even the canopy of the four-poster made me feel like I was being shielded, protected from above.

I don't know when exactly I drifted off, but something pulled me out of my sleep with a start. A tapping sound.

Tap.   **Tap.**   **Tap.**

GEORGE does a thumbs-up over his shoulder at SID, who looks confused but smiles.

The room was faintly washed with moonlight coming in from the window. I sat up and instantly turned on the bedside lamp. The room looked exactly as it had the night before. Then something caught my eye. A shadow shifted in the moonlight coming through the gap in the curtains. I slid cautiously from the covers and stepped across the room. I pulled back the curtain to see – the branch of a tree. Was this what had been tapping? As if to answer, a gust blew the branch against the glass. But the sound that had woke me had been different, harsher. Or had it? The branch rapped the window again. I wracked my memory trying to recall the first sound but only heard the tapping of the branch... But hadn't my first instinct been to look towards the corridor...?

I tried to remember. Was it from the door?

Tap in left ear.

Or the window?

Tap in right ear.

The door?

Tap in left ear.

The window....

Tap in right ear.

I couldn't be sure. I almost wanted to hear the ominous, original sound again – nothing.

I steadied myself, and nearly laughed at my nervousness as I climbed back into bed. One night in an old house and already so skittish? As I nestled myself under the duvet, the branch tapped on the window again and –

The mic boom swings by itself again and hits the wall with a thump. GEORGE *turns uneasily at the sound… but the studio looks the same.*

– and I told myself once, then twice, that it was certainly what I'd heard.

* * *

GEORGE *agitatedly sips some water, looks around, shakes it off, then continues.*

I woke up the next morning not knowing when I'd last slept so well, and thinking how ludicrous my nighttime worries now felt. I threw open the curtains and gasped. The blizzard had finally come, and transformed the valley below into an image of festive perfection.

I spent some time wandering around, wiping down the surfaces, and clearing away my father's place at the kitchen table. If I was going to be here for the next few days, I wanted it to feel like my own space.

Eventually, I sat down at the desk in the parlour and started working through the stacks upon stacks of papers. I knew it would be faster if I just bundled them all together and burned them. Yet the hope that I might discover something about my father meant I gave every single one of them at least a quick glance. It was slow, slow work. I found an invoice from Mr Morrison and smirked when I saw how much he charged. Clearly not quite the unthinking business-relic he'd first appeared. Beyond this, just bills and bank statements – nothing that revealed anything about what kind of man my father was.

Three hours passed. I stretched; my back cracked in protest at my posture. Then I scooped up the perused papers and tossed them into the grate. The flames swallowed them greedily.

The recording light flares, gently.

After lunch, and with a coffee in hand, I stepped
into the library, positioned myself in the
armchair with my feet up on the wooden stool.
I scrolled over the headlines: all so terrible, but
pleasantly faraway.

My mind wandered to her again. If she and I had
stayed together, we could have made a life for
ourselves here. The thought of little versions
of us skidding around the library, their giggles
bouncing through the house, almost made me
smile.

I sat up quickly. My thumb had been hovering
over her number. I hesitated. My gaze rested
on the cracked mirror. I flicked down to Mr
Morrison's number instead. Worth asking,
I thought. He might help me better understand
his former employer, or what the blue corridor
meant. Two rings. My eyes fixed on my fractured
reflection. One more ring, then –

'What's wrong?'

'Nothing's wrong,' I snapped back.

'Are you sure?'

I felt a flash of frustration at his lack of faith.
'Yes, I am sure. I just wanted to ask something
about my – ' I paused for a moment, and
wondered what my father had told him about
me. He'd probably told him that I hadn't
amounted to much. I bit my lip and switched
questions.

'My dad wanted the house to be pulled down
correct?'

'Yes.'

'Well, most of his – um – possessions come to
me?'

'Hm.'

'Well, what would – what would the process
of – '

'Would it be possible for you to keep the house
instead of it being demolished?'

'Yes.'

'I can have a look, but your father was very clear
that he wanted the house gutted, torn down and
then sell off the land.'

I wouldn't be fobbed off so easily. 'I know. But,
can you look into it at least,' I said with what
I felt was a tone of steely authority.

A pause, then –

'Let me know how you feel in a few days.' He
hung up.

What a weird, rude man. Yet my impulsive
request started to settle in my mind – what if
I did stay here? The seclusion would be beautiful,
productive. Yes, I could see that future. Wipe
away the remnants of my father's possessions
and make this house my own. And no need for
any screaming toddlers to ruin the seclusion.
I stooped to pick up the dust cloth and,
balancing on the stool, reached up to reattach
the fabric to the top of the mirror, blocking out
its splintered surface.

I could give it a few days just to keep Morrison
from freaking out. Yet it was certainly better here
than where I was before. I kept thinking this to
myself again and again throughout the rest of the
day, until I eventually curled up under the duvet
and turned out the light.

* * *

Tap.   **Tap.**   **Tap.**

I sat up instantly. The bedroom was still. Yet every part of me was alert. I was certain, certain that I'd heard that noise again. I breathed as lightly as possible so that my ears could scour the silence for any –

Tap.

There. And this time I was sure that it wasn't the branch against the window, but was coming from the corridor and –

Tap.   **Tap.**

And getting closer. The certainty of that sunk in slowly. I held my breath and stared towards the door. Had I locked it before going to sleep? I wasn't sure if –

Tap.   **Tap.**

It was coming nearer and nearer, and there was also something else. A resounding thump.

Thump.   **Thump.**   **Thump.**

The sound was so close now, but then – silence. I stayed frozen. Ears straining to hear where it had gone. Hoping that maybe it would have passed and I'd hear it fading away to the distance. Then on the door itself, three heavy –

THUMP.   **THUMP.**   **THUMP.**

I gripped the edge of the bed tightly. There was no one there. There couldn't be. Yet I didn't dare move closer. The fear tightened around my neck like a rope. Unable to bear the anticipation any longer, I edged slowly, towards the door. 'Hello? Anybody here?' The door knob was cold to my grip. For a moment I thought it was vibrating in my hand, before I realised that I was shaking. Inhale, and –

Open. I stared into the gloom determined to find the source of the noise, yet also fearing anything that might break the oppressive stillness. I stretched for the light switch, and flicked it. The lights illuminated one long empty corridor. I almost laughed with relief I was alone in this quiet empty house.

But. A very soft sound –

Step.   **Step.**

– almost like someone trying to creep away without making any noise. Yet as soon as I moved to follow, the footsteps quickened. Coming from above? No, ahead. A light patter. I crept along as quietly as possible, but the steps were already on the tiny staircase ahead.

Step.   **Step.**   **Step.**

I paused and stared up to the shadowy landing above. I had only been upstairs in the light of day...

I hit the switch and the bulbs flared, casting away the shadows. I reached the landing and listened, trying to block out the sound of the blood pumping in my ears. Nothing. But as I shifted my weight forward the steps pattered away from me as though whatever it was knew it was being pursued. I couldn't see anything, but I moved faster down the corridor until I reached –

Suddenly, two booms mics swing down from the ceiling straight at GEORGE, *who ducks just in time, and turns.*

GEORGE	Ah!
SID	(*looking up*) You good?
GEORGE	Yeah, no. Just. The things fell off the –
SID	Nah way.

GEORGE	Exactly when –
SID	I'm coming through.

SID *disappears, he pushes at the door. But it's locked.*

GEORGE	Sid. Sid. Still recording.

But it's sound proofed. GEORGE *knocks on the glass.*

The door's sealed. You're still recording.

SID *reappears, having not heard.*

SID	(*into the mic*) The door's sealed. We're still recording.

GEORGE *rolls his eyes.*

GEORGE	I'll just –

The recording light turns off, and SID *disappears then enters the space.*

SID	What's up?
GEORGE	The booms came off.
SID	Wow, yeah. New studio. Dash job. I'll let them know.

SID *pushes the fallen booms back into place.*

Shoddy, shoddy stuff.

GEORGE	But it happened just when –
SID	When?
GEORGE	In the story.
SID	Cosmic vibrations.
GEORGE	What?
SID	Tiny earthquake.
GEORGE	Stop it.

SID	You spooked, bro?
	Beat.
GEORGE	No.
SID	You are. Ah, I love that. Getting into the spirit of it. Big vibe.
GEORGE	Yeah. Shall we –
SID	Yeah, yeah, yeah. I can do a sneaky stitch job. Wanna pick up from… 'I couldn't see anything but – '
GEORGE	Sure, sure.
SID	All right?
GEORGE	Yep.
SID	Not feeling the heeby –
GEORGE	Let's crack on.
SID	Aite-y tight-y. Three… Two… One…
	GEORGE *shakes it off, and picks up the story from where he got to.*
GEORGE	I couldn't see anything but –
	GEORGE *repeats to try and get his head back in the game.*
	I moved faster down the corridor until I reached the corner.
	Click.
	It sounded like something metal clicking into place, but I couldn't tell what had made the sound. There was no doorway nearby, just panel after panel of peeling wallpaper. Yet my mouth hung open as I stared at the walls. What had seemed grey during the day, now appeared a shimmering blue in the light of the moon.

I stood still as I marvelled at the gleaming blue corridor.

After a moment, I pushed my hair out of my eyes. My forehead was beaded with sweat. What was I doing? Chasing noises in the night. There was probably some poor rat that I'd scared and it was now trembling in its hiding place. Nothing else.

Yet just to be sure, just to calm myself, I walked room to room turning every light on until there wasn't a shadow remaining. It was only when I stretched out on my bed that I realised how quickly I was breathing, as if I'd been running. I closed my eyes, listening to the now-quiet house, and wished for sleep.

* * *

SID   (*in a creepy voice through the headphones*) Geeeeoorrrgggeee… Geeeoooorrrgggeee….

GEORGE   …yes…?

SID   Loving your work.

               GEORGE *smiles, then continues.*

GEORGE   (*adjusting*)

I felt slightly sheepish as I left my bedroom the next morning so it took me a moment to notice that none of the lights were working. I flicked a few switches before realising that leaving all the lights on had, unsurprisingly, blown a fuse. Knowing I deserved this petty punishment, I followed my father's meticulous instructions from the letter and sure enough the power was back. Yet still a bit annoyed at myself, I threw a coat on and strode outside to fill my lungs with the cool, winter air.

It was like stepping out to a Christmas postcard. The snow was even thicker than I'd thought and I was already out of breath after a minute of stamping along the drive. The intensity of the blizzard meant there was no choice but to stay put for the next few days. I abandoned my plan of going to look at the condition of the road, and veered back to stomp around the house instead.

Just ahead of me protruding out of a snowbank I noticed a gnarled stick. It took a few vigorous twists before I eventually snapped it off. The crack was far louder than I'd expected. I looked around, almost as if someone might tell me off, yet there was only the white expanse staring back at me.

Gnarled stick in hand, I looped round the house twice more until my teeth started to chatter so headed inside to warm up. I stamped the snow from my shoes, and was about to go upstairs when I paused, holding the stick in both hands, almost reverently, as a thought scratched at my mind. I then walked quickly over to the wall and tapped it lightly. It predictably made the sound of a small stick hitting a big wooden panel, but not similar to what I'd heard during the night. I tapped a few more walls, with the same result. I had to know, even if it meant hitting the stick against every surface in the house. I walked up the stairs, bouncing the stick harshly on every spindle of the bannister. The sound was heavier but still didn't have the same quality as what I thought I'd heard. Or did it? I wasn't sure. In a flash of frustration, I threw the stick down the stairs and it clattered to the stone floor below. The sound echoed after me as I hurried to my room.

Once I was in dry clothes and heading back down the staircase, I saw the stick still lying

forlornly on the flagstones. I felt so frustrated
at myself for the absurdity of tapping it against
the wall that I picked it up and broke it into
two, then three, then four before rushing into
the library and dumping it into the fireplace.
I smiled as I got the flames going and the stick
became just another piece of kindling in the
grate.

The red recording light flickers; GEORGE
doesn't notice.

The fire brightened my mood, so I felt ready to
tackle the endless books which lined the shelves.
It felt wrong throwing so much literature into
a skip, yet if I was going to stay here, it would
be good to free up some space for my own
modest collection. And maybe there might
be inspiration for a new essay, something that
would prove to everyone who mattered that
I was worthy of tenure, or at least employment,
after all.

Most of the heavily thumbed paperbacks
I chucked into a pile without looking at them.
I took more time with each of the embossed
books. Some of the most beautiful were
completely untouched, and cracked when
I opened them as though no one had ever prised
apart their covers before to see what was inside.
As I pulled a particularly ornate volume down,
something fluttered to the floor.

I thought for a moment it had come from the
book I was holding, but it was a good way to my
left and I couldn't see how it had fallen that far.
I looked around but everything seemed as settled
as before. Yet there it was: a creased piece of
paper on the claret-coloured carpet.

I turned it over and saw that it was an oddly
posed photograph of a man and a young boy.

A father and a son. But not me. My dad and his
father. I'd never seen a photo of my grandfather
before. He had a proud face, high cheekbones.
And his eyes glared at the camera as though
he was angry at the photographer for the
presumption of daring to take his picture.

I'd spent so much time fixed on the idea of my
father here as an old man, that I'd forgotten
he'd grown up in this house with his father. This
stern looking man whose hand gripped the little
shoulder, keeping his son firmly in position.
There was so little I'd known about my father, his
family and now it was too late to ask…

I readjusted my jumper, which felt cloying. I then
slid the photo into a book that I left on its side
on a shelf. I stepped back and even though the
shadows had started to lengthen in the room,
I could admire the moderate dent I'd made
clearing this section. Five wooden shelves were
exposed like ribs along one wall.

I went back and forward to the skip, dumping
armful after armful of unwanted books inside.
By the time I'd finished, a gloom had descended
on the library so I hit the light switch, and saw
something move out of the corner of my eye.
I looked round but everything in the room
was still. I turned the lights off, then on again
and saw the same flicker of – something on
the stained wall behind the empty shelves – an
odd-shaped shadow descending from the beam
above. Yet as I blinked it was gone. I shivered.
The room suddenly felt arctic. I stared up at
the central beam which still had the same score
marks in the middle yet otherwise was just plain
wood. I looked back to the wall and determined
to keep my eyes fixed on the exact spot, I turned
the lamp off once more, steadied myself, then
turned it on. This time I was sure. The outline of

the beam was still on the wall, but coming down from the centre was the shadow of a rope and at the end of the rope was a loop. I glanced at the real beam above me – there wasn't anything hanging from it. I stared at the wall and saw –

Suddenly, a real noose drops from the ceiling of the studio. GEORGE *moves out of the way and — the studio plunges into darkness.*

Lights. The noose is gone.

An echo of GEORGE*'s last line of the story.*

SID	You good?
GEORGE	Yeah, I – I thought I saw it for a sec.
SID	What?
GEORGE	(*trying to laugh it off*) A noose.
SID	You saw the noose?
GEORGE	I mean, obviously not. Must've been the lights or... But for a moment, I thought I saw a noose swing down.
SID	Incredible.
GEORGE	What?
SID	...this, um, bit, man. It's so powerful bro.
GEORGE	(*still slightly unsettled, looking strangely at* SID) Right.
SID	This is the real stuff. It's sounding great. Pick up from 'I stared at the wall and saw...'
GEORGE	Yep.
SID	Houston we're blasting off again in: Three... Two... One...

GEORGE *smiles, recentres, then begins to speak.*

GEORGE I stared at the wall and saw – nothing. I kept flicking the light off and on, off and on, but the shadow didn't return. I rubbed my eyes, and nearly jumped at an ominous rumble from my stomach. I realised I hadn't eaten anything all day.

I went to the kitchen, ripped the lid off a tin of soup and drank it straight from the can. I was shaking so much that the liquid dripped down my chin and splattered on the floor below. I wiped my mouth with the back of my hand, and tried to breathe as my mind kept racing with thoughts of the shadow, but also of the photo...

The image of my grandfather – the stare, the severe expression, the hand gripping the shoulder: it unnerved me. Yet for some reason my dad had still felt the urge to come back to his father's house. To give up everything he had and stay here in lonely luxury. But was it luxury? The library was nice, yes. Yet looking around the plain kitchen, it didn't have the feel of an especially decadent lifestyle. Then my mind shifted to the image of the single bed in his stark bedroom.

Why choose to sleep in that bare room?' Why not live like a duke in one of the grander suites, rather than hiding away in a forgotten corner of the...

I let the tin of soup clatter to the floor.

Had my father heard the same noises I heard and taken shelter up there to be as far from them as possible?

If that was true, then why not leave? Why endure it in a little box room, like a prisoner serving out a –

thump   ***thump***   ***thump***

A muffled noise came from above. Like someone sprinting along the corridor, followed by a heavy dull thumping sound. Yet it was hard to make out. I carefully opened the kitchen; there was only silence. I waited for a moment in the darkness. And then from the far end of the hallway came a quick series of bangs –

bang   **bang**

And a final resounding crash.

crash

– as if something heavy had fallen down the staircase. I ran through the hallway, turned at the bottom of the stairs and –

No debris, no loose tiles, nothing to explain where the sound had come from. There was enough moonlight to see that the steps were completely clear. Yet I was certain something, someone, had fallen down the stairs.

I shivered. The darkness had got to me again. I flicked one switch, the light fixtures on the wall lit up.

The studio brightens.

That was better. I pressed another, and the bulbs on the floor above turned on.

The studio brightens again.

I felt my mood lift with the growing brightness. I flicked the third switch – every light went out.

The studio darkens. GEORGE *frowns, but carries on.*

Stupid fuses. I scrabbled for my phone and turned on the torch.

Its pathetically small beam shone around.

Hoping that the fuse box wouldn't be too difficult to navigate in the darkness, I headed towards the –

Creak.

My heart was in my throat as I snapped back round to the stairs, yet there wasn't anything there. It had sounded like a wooden ratchet being –

Creak.

I turned quickly and saw the door of the library swinging on its hinges. Had I left it open earlier? Yes, yes surely. And now there it was, just blowing in a draught. But – I still couldn't bring myself to move towards it. Every part of me wanted to run up the stairs and lock myself in my room. Or call Mr Morrison. Or – No, I was being stupid. The lights going off had freaked me out and I, and I – had to get a grip of myself.

Creak.

The door shifted again. With an effort I didn't believe myself capable of, I took one step, then another, towards it. There was a red glow inside the library from the remains of the fire. I reached the threshold, gave the door a slight push and it swung wide open.

The red recording light pulses once.

I held my phone torch high to try and see as much of the room as I could.

And saw that the mirror was uncovered and on the floor lay a crumpled figure. No, no – the dust sheet. The dust sheet had just slipped off and fallen into a heap. The exposed mirror reflected back a cracked version of the room and the eerie red glow.

The red recording light pulses again.

As I stooped to pick up the fallen fabric,
something shifted in the corner of my vision.
I stood upright but only saw my own reflection in
the broken mirror. The pulsing glow of embers did
make it feel like the room was moving, wavering.

*The red recording light pulses softly and
continuously.*

Yet I thought – I thought there'd been
something else. Something closer to me. I walked
towards the mirror. The eyes of my reflected self
were stretched wide, but everything in the room
stayed still.

I was nearly ready to turn away, when something
made my blood go cold.

Breath.

A breath on the back of my neck. My spine
trembled as I felt it again.

Breath.

Someone was behind me. Directly behind me.
I froze in anticipation of a blow, but none came.
Just –

'There you are.'

*The face of the figure appears in the
glass behind* GEORGE. *He turns and
screams.*

Moment of darkness.

Again, an echo of GEORGE's *last line of
the story.*

The lights adjust as SID *turns on his lamp
and we see him alone in the booth.*

GEORGE   What'd you do to the lights?

SID   The lights?

GEORGE   They just –

SID	It was only my lamp, bro.
GEORGE	Then, then –
SID	What's going on, man?
GEORGE	What?
SID	Why are you twitching out like this?
GEORGE	I'm not, I – I –
SID	Are you sure you can get through this?
GEORGE	What?
SID	Finish this? Because if you're feeling strung out – I wanna make sure you can make it all the way –
GEORGE	I'm fine. It's just the story.
SID	Heavy, right?
GEORGE	Yeah.
SID	I did warn you.
	Uncomfortable silence.
GEORGE	Did you?
SID	Course. Trigger warnings, ha… Shall we go again?
GEORGE	Yep.
SID	Sure?
GEORGE	Yep, yes.
SID	Umm, so…. 'My eyes opened. I looked back into the mirror and saw…'
	GEORGE *just nods.*
	Rolling.
	GEORGE *opens his eyes, looks to the screen and restarts the story.*

GEORGE

My eyes opened. I looked back into the mirror and saw... A face. A gaunt, grey face which grinned at me. I snapped round. The room was deserted. Everything was in its proper place: the books, the chair, the stool. I held my breath. But still, nothing. I slowly turned back to the mirror to my own fearful reflection staring back at me.

Yet I couldn't take my eyes from the mirror and just peered into the depths of the reflected room. My eyes flicking from shadow to shadow, as if my watching could somehow stop the figure reappearing. Nothing moved though, except for the faint swirl of snowflakes buffeting against the glass of the windows. The only sound was the distant moan of the wind.

Eventually I tore myself from my vigil and closed the library door behind me. Yet the image of the face stayed with me, and, as I walked up the stairs, I realised what it reminded me of: a similar expression, a similar hate-filled stare. In a photo. The photo of my dad and – his father.

I stopped and looked back towards the closed library door. Every part of me wanted to continue upstairs, wrap myself in the duvet and forget about this whole day. But. But, the photo of my grandfather. I'd left it in the book on the shelf. It could wait until morning, surely? No. I knew I had to check. I headed back downstairs, gripped the handle of the library door, took a breath, twisted and pushed it open.

The shadows in the room had grown as the embers in the grate burned lower and lower.

The red recording light pulses; the brightness fading each time.

I lifted my phone torch high and took a step. Everything was still. I carefully approached the exposed shelves, and found the book I'd left on its side. I picked it up and flicked through. It was empty. I held it for a moment, as cold confusion seeped through me. I knew, I knew I'd left the photo in there. I turned through every page again, then in a fit of frustration threw the book away from me and it skidded across the floor.

'Now, why would you do that?'

I twisted round but there was no one there. Just the empty shelves and the exposed wall.

'We'll have to hang you high so you learn your lesson.'

The gloom in the far corner was so thick, so dark that I couldn't make out anything. Yet I was certain that someone was standing there, just beyond the reach of the light.

'Hello?' I called out. I tried to hide the tremor in my voice, 'Any– anybody here?' Silence. I glanced to my right and the open door to the hallway –

The door to the studio opens by itself; GEORGE *doesn't see…*

– then, then back to the shadowy corner. I inched towards it. With each step, my breath caught in my throat. I dreaded what I was about to see. Then the torchlight reached the walls and – an empty corner. I exhaled, relieved beyond words. But then, I heard an all too familiar sound.

Tap.

I snapped my head round to the mirror and for a moment I couldn't understand what I was seeing. Instead of my own reflection, there was a shadowy figure was on the other side of the cracked glass, inside the reflection with its hand pressed up against the surface of the –

Tap.

A flair of red light in the doorway to reveal… a shadowy figure outside the room. GEORGE doesn't see.

Its hand made contact with the glass once more –

Tap.

Another flair of red light in the doorway. The shadowy figure is closer. GEORGE still does not notice.

– right against the cracks. As I stared, I saw its head tilt in my direction and a smile spread across its face. The hand came towards the glass once more, then passed through the surface and into the room –

The lights flair once more. GEORGE turns to see… nothing. The doorway is empty. GEORGE backs away from the door towards the edge of the studio. His eyes fixed on the door.

THEN – from the wall behind him, an arm bursts out and grabs for GEORGE's face.

Blackout.

GEORGE   Stop! Stop.

The lights restore. GEORGE is alone. The door is closed. GEORGE wrenches off his headphone. SID turns the recording light off, and enters.

SID   We're not gonna get this done, if you keep –

GEORGE   There was someone here.

SID	Where?
GEORGE	And the door opened, then – then –
SID	But it's been locked the whole –
GEORGE	And an arm came from here –
SID	An arm?
GEORGE	– caught me –
SID	You got caught on something?
GEORGE	(*like a lost child*) I – I – I don't know.
	Pause.
SID	Use it.
GEORGE	Use what?
SID	You're tired and the story's getting to you. But that's exactly what they wanted: to hear your real fear.
GEORGE	I'm not sure I can –
SID	Finish? I mean, sure bro. You do you. But they'll just get someone else y'know.
GEORGE	I can give it a go another day.
SID	They want this by tomorrow.
GEORGE	I know.
SID	You were the one who was late.
GEORGE	I know.
SID	And you're desperate for the work.
GEORGE	I'm not desperate –
SID	No, sure. But, as a mate, I reckon it'd be good to take a breath, channel whatever ride you're on right now and finish the recording. Yeah?

GEORGE   (*exhale*) Yep, yep.

SID *returns to the booth and flips on the recording light.*

GEORGE *steadies himself, then carries on.*

The hand came towards the glass once more, then passed through the surface and into the room itself. I ran. Ran towards the open door. I thought I could hear the steps of the figure behind me, but I didn't turn to find out. I sprinted up the staircase. My phone swung in my hand; its torch cast light and shadows in disorientating waves in front of me. I turned along the corridor, my heart beating in my ears. Reached my bedroom, burst inside and slammed the door behind me. Turning the key in the lock.

I collapsed with my back pressed against the door. Each breath felt like my lungs would rip out of my throat. I strained to hear if any sound was coming from the corridor. The wind still blew against the window, but otherwise the house was silent.

I didn't have the strength to stand, so I dragged myself away from the door. My eyes fixed on the handle. I pressed my back against the wall opposite, my head under the windowsill and waited. Time stretched by. But with each minute that passed I started to calm myself, just a little.

I had to get out of here. But navigating my way through the snow in the darkness was impossible. I didn't want my frozen corpse to be found when the snow eventually thawed. Or I could wait until morning. I'd stand a better chance if I could see my way through the snow, or – No. There was only one thing I could do. I picked up my phone and called Mr Morrison. He answered instantly.

'What's wrong?'

'I – I – think my grandfather's in the house.'

'Impossible. Your grandfather died long before you were born.'

'But – I – I – '

'You're going to be okay. I'll come now.'

'The roads?'

'It'll be slow, but I'll try.'

'What happened here? What did my grandfather do to my dad…?'

'I…'

'Tell me. Please.'

'Don't tell tales to others.'

The voice came from the phone itself.

'Disappointing. You were always so disappointing.'

With a jolt, I threw the phone across the room and it cracked into the wall opposite. It wasn't his voice. He wasn't here. I knew he couldn't be here.

I pressed my back even harder against the wall. The stillness of the house made me more nervous. I wanted to hear the pipes, or a creak or anything. Yet the whole building just stood on edge, waiting.

I stared at the door. I knew it was my fearful mind but it looked as if it was ready to burst open and release whatever was on other side. I stared, and stared but it stayed still.

Then from above my head –

Tap.

I looked up, yet it was just the branch against the window. I felt relieved, but as I turned back to the room, I saw that the locked door was now – open. Opened into the corridor beyond. Like an invitation. Every part of my brain told me to close it. Shut it tight. Lock it. And wait for Mr Morrison.

But somewhere within, like an itch, was the idea that maybe, maybe the sounds would lead me to the truth, to some understanding of what happened here all those years ago.

I stooped by the doorway to pick up my cracked phone. The torch still worked and even though its dull glow didn't spread far, it was comforting all the same. I stepped into the corridor and looked from one side to the other.

The house was silent: no guiding footsteps, no tapping, no voices. I waited for a moment, my eyes trying to see beyond the edge of the torchlight's reach. Only stillness. I then remembered back to when I'd followed the footsteps, when it had been like someone was fleeing in the shadows. I looked at the glow from my phone. I inhaled, then turned off my torch and waited.

It's almost pitch-black in the studio. We only hear GEORGE's breaths.

A sliver of moonlight illuminated the space but otherwise it was completely dark.

Then, footsteps. Soft, light footsteps coming closer. I closed my eyes and waited for their approach. I thought whatever it was would collide with me, but instead the footsteps went past me and the sound disappeared at the end of the corridor.

But then a voice in my ear –

'Out of bed so late. I will have to teach you a lesson.'

The sound of a rope being unfurled, then whipped against the wall.

Whoosh   and   Thump.

'You will learn not to disappoint me.'

I ran. The heavy footfall followed me. The sound of the noose bouncing off the wall.

Thump.   Thump.   Thump.

I turned a corner, then another and found myself at the top of the staircase with the hall in darkness below me. I stopped –

'No, Papa, no.'

'I'll string you high.'

'Let go of me.'

'So high until you learn to behave better.'

'LET GO!'

A tumble, crashes of something heavy falling down the stairs, and a final sickening crack as whatever it was hit the stone floor below. Then silence.

'Papa?'

I peered down as if expecting to see a crumpled body in the hall below, but could only see the hard stone floor.

I went down one step. Then another. Trying to see anything, anything at all, but my eyes couldn't pierce the darkness. I took one more step then froze.

There was something at the bottom of the stairs. I blinked once, hoping that the image would disappear.

A flash of light with each blink.

It was still there: bent into the strangest shape, yet unmistakably the body of a man. I blinked again and shook my head.

Flash.

But I could still see it below. Both legs sprawled out at awkward angles, an arm bent back on itself, and the jaw twisted to one side, the neck broken. I closed my eyes once again and –

Flash. Yet standing next to GEORGE is THE FIGURE. It reaches out a hand to grasp his shoulder. A screech reaches fever pitch then –

Blackout.

The lights return and THE FIGURE is gone.

GEORGE	I'm done. We're done.
SID	(*in the booth*) Still recording, bro.
GEORGE	There was someone here, next to me and – I don't care about the money. I don't know if it's me or here or whatever but I'm finished, finished with this.
SID	Come on, you're nearly there.
GEORGE	Tell them to find someone else for their stupid story, I'm through.
SID	No.
GEORGE	Open the door.
SID	It's sealed.
GEORGE	So stop the recording and unseal it.
SID	I'm not going to do that.
GEORGE	What?

SID   I'm sorry.

               A moment.

GEORGE   (*softly, unsettled*) Sid, come on. Let me
               out.

SID   So you heard the tapping?

GEORGE   What tapping?

SID   You said you heard a tapping, right?

GEORGE   In the headphones, yeah.

SID   There was no tapping in the
               headphones.

GEORGE   But – but you showed me at the
               beginning, all the sound effects and –

SID   That was just a few creaking doors and
               gusty winds. But no tapping.

GEORGE   And the voice?

SID   No voices either. And did you see a grey
               figure?

               Beat.

GEORGE   What's going on? Open this door right
               now.

SID   I'm not opening the door. You're staying
               there.

GEORGE   Sid!

SID   This story has been around, in one
               version or another for years – details get
               tweaked, but always when you read it or
               hear it – the ghost – his ghost – latches
               onto you. And the only way to get rid of it
               is to pass it on. Tell the story to someone
               else…

GEORGE   What if I don't?

SID	He stays with you. He's not always there but you'll hear his tapping, getting closer and closer, then he'll start to appear.
GEORGE	I...I...
SID	Listen, bro –
GEORGE	Don't 'bro' me
SID	I can see you're upset –
GEORGE	Oh, for –
SID	But I need to make sure. You saw a noose drop from above, right?
GEORGE	...
SID	Have you seen that?
GEORGE	Please, open the door Sid.
SID	Have you seen a noose drop in front of you?
GEORGE	Yes.
SID	Then you've got it now.
GEORGE	I don't want it.
SID	I – can't live with it anymore. He starts appearing more when, if...
GEORGE	...if?
SID	If you're about to have a kid.
GEORGE	But –
SID	I let my brother tell me the story because he was gonna have his first, which was huge as – cos our dad passed when we were little, so we never had a... and I thought I could live with it, especially as I didn't want to have any myself, but – but then Sasha got pregnant, and we wanted to keep it. As, even without

	knowing how to, I realised I wanted to be a dad, and – and…
GEORGE	(*pleading*) Sid.
SID	The closer it gets to the due date… I've been seeing him more and more… and, I'm barely keeping it steady, then…
GEORGE	Then, what?
SID	I started to see a tiny body… Dangling. From a rope. And I know it's my boy. It was an outline at first, but then becomes clearer the nearer we get to when he's supposed to arrive…
GEORGE	Please, Sid.
SID	I'm sorry. I thought of every option and you felt like the right choice.
GEORGE	Why?
SID	It only gets really bad when a baby is on the way and you don't want –
GEORGE	That doesn't mean that –
SID	Listen.
GEORGE	– just because you're having a –
SID	Hey.
GEORGE	Then I'm stuck with it, then I have to live with it.
SID	But…why do you think we're recording this?

Pause.

GEORGE *looks at the microphone, the studio, as the the truth about why he is there finally sinks in.*

GEORGE	No, no – that's –
SID	It's the only way.

GEORGE	You can't – what if I change my mind?
SID	You'll have the recording and can choose what to do with it.
GEORGE	Hold on. There must be another –
SID	I'll be back in the morning.
GEORGE	I'll call for help.

SID *holds up* GEORGE*'s phone.*

I'll – I'll scream, someone will –

SID	Fully sound-proofed room.
GEORGE	(*a barely audible moan*)
SID	Finish the story. Then you can pass the recording onto someone else. When they see the noose swing down – you know it's passed on. I've given you a way to free yourself of it, which is more than what I had…

SID *leaves.* GEORGE *is alone.*

GEORGE	Sid, Sid… SID!!

GEORGE *hits the door, then turns and – SCREAMS. But we can't hear him. The sound   disappears and all we can see is* GEORGE *screaming silently into the void.*

GEORGE *stops yelling, and starts panting. We can hear this again. He's looking around for a way out when –*

Tap.

No, no, no, no.

Tap.

Please, no.

Breaths on the neck. Steady, threatening.

I'm sorry. I'm so sorry.

GEORGE *lets out a whimper, inhales, then continues...*

Then its head cracked round and smiled up the stairs at me. As the figure pushed itself up from the stone floor, it sounded as if every bone was snapping under the effort to reach its full height. Then I saw, dangling from its right hand, a length of rope with a noose at the end.

'That wasn't very nice. Was it?'

It beat the noose on every step as it climbed. I stood frozen by the sight.

Thump.   Thump.   Thump.

As it got closer, I could finally see its face. The grey skin stretched over a skull as though the bone beneath was trying to burst through. Its whole body twitched sharply with each step it took. The thin lips parted in a vicious smile.

'I don't want to hurt you, just stay very still.'

Thump.   Thump.   Thump.

I couldn't move. It was six steps, five steps away.

'Now, let's put this round your neck.'

It reached towards my throat.

Then the feeling of a small, warm hand which slipped into mine and pulled, giving me the strength to turn – and run.

'Come Back Here.'

Thump.   Thump.   Thump.

I fled along the corridor, turned a corner and ran past door after door to the staircase at the back of the house. I sprinted up the rickety steps, aware the whole time of the constant –

Thump.   **Thump.**   **Thump.**

– behind me.

Along the top floor, round the corner and into
the glimmering blue corridor, and the dead end.
The thumping beat of the noose was getting
closer. But then, one of the panels in the wall
swung open to reveal a small space beyond.
I burst in and pushed the panel closed behind
me. I pressed my back hard against it and felt the
tremors in my spine.

'Where are you?'

The rope started to crash into the walls of the
corridor. One swing made contact with the panel
behind me and my whole body shuddered with
the impact, but then I heard it crash against
the wall on the other side, then from further
and further away. Its distant, directionless rage
made me think I might be safe in here, for the
moment.

I stared around the hidden chamber I was in.
It took a moment for my eyes to adjust to the
gloom but then I saw on every inch of every wall
were words, scored deeply into the wood.

*Phrases appear in the gleaming blue UV
light on the walls of the studio around
GEORGE, as though scratched into the
surfaces.*

I stared at the scratches of a trapped child. So it
took me a moment to see that at my feet was a
small wooden box. The sort of thing a young boy
would keep his little treasures in. On top of it
was a note scribbled in my father's handwriting
saying simply, 'For my son. Please make sure this
finds him.'

I knelt down, flicked the brass catch and lifted
the lid. Inside were countless pieces of paper of

different sizes. Photos of me as a child. Clippings from a school newspaper. An article I'd written for a magazine. My hand trembled as I sifted through them. There was so much, an archive of my entire life, that I almost didn't see the letter addressed to me which was on the underside of the lid. I picked it up. I traced my thumb over the familiar blue writing. Then, I slowly turned the envelope and opened it.

'My son,

I know this letter will not make up for the words I never said to you in person. I was so determined to not be as terrible a parent as my father that I forgot to even try to be a decent dad for you. Yet I hope by the time you've finished this, you'll understand that everything I've done has been to protect you.

You did not know my father and all the better for it. He was a cruel, vicious man who knew no pleasure except the brutalisation of others. When I was seven, my mother passed. I lost my shield and became the sole target of his viciousness. We were alone in his house together. On the rare occasions of visitors, he was always his most effortlessly charming. I knew the punishment if I'd have asked them for help, so I tried to plead for salvation with my eyes. Yet they all didn't, or chose not to see.

Whenever his mood turned, I would run to the one place he couldn't find me: my hidden chamber behind the wall. Because if he did get hold of me, he'd drag me to the library, tie a noose round my neck, loop it over the beam and then make me stand on a stool he'd had made specially. He'd ratchet the seat slowly down to the point where the rope strained tight and my toes barely kept contact with its surface. He watched me from his chair so I never fell, but I was kept suspended there in a horrific pirouette until he grew bored. When I was let down I collapsed at his feet, begging for forgiveness which he never gave me.

Once I was sent away to board, it was a relief. No matter how brutal my teachers were it was nothing compared to what I endured at home. One winter when I returned, he was worse than he'd ever been before. Following me around the corridors, bouncing the rope off the walls. One night, he chased me to the top of the staircase, yet I slipped his grasp and he fell the full length of the stairs, breaking his neck on the floor below.

I was relieved by his death. I finally felt free of him. I moved away. I grew up. I met your mother. I knew peace. I knew love. Then you came along and I've never known a feeling like it. I adored you entirely. Yet I was consumed by a fear that I would drop and break the delicate little creature in my arms. And that's when I started seeing him again. Every time I looked at myself in a mirror, I only saw him. Leering at my new happiness, determined to destroy it.

I couldn't expose you to his monstrous presence, or what his presence did to me. He was always strongest when I was near you. So eventually I left and locked myself away in his old house to protect you in the only way I knew how. My one hope is that his memory dies with me. I was always his plaything in life and I hope my death ends his obsession forever.

I held off on sending this to you until I knew that his house and everything linked to him had been destroyed. I cannot allow what he did to have any chance of being passed onto you.

I have loved watching you grow and flourish from afar, and, if there is any life after this one, then I will continue to watch over you when I'm gone.

I am so proud of you. Now and always.

Your loving Father.

The last few words were blotted by the tears which fell from my eyes. I looked up to the ceiling but didn't try to blink them away. I just let them flow. Years of feelings held tight in a fist, finally released. I whispered, 'I'm so sorry, Dad. I never knew. I – I forgive you.'

Then there was a sound, like the exhalation of a house finally letting out a breath.

After what could have been an hour or an eternity, I heard Mr Morrison calling my name below. I stepped cautiously out of my father's hideaway with the box under my arm, and checked both ways before heading towards the stairs. Yet as I rounded the corner, I froze.

Tap.

I didn't dare to turn round, but couldn't bring myself to move forward.

Tap.

Then a ratcheting...

Creak.

And a creak of something swinging from a rope.

Flash: visible for a moment in the booth, a small child-like figure suspended from a noose. In a moment, it's gone.

I just ran, almost falling down the stairs, before colliding with Mr Morrison on the landing. I held him close and wept. He didn't say anything, but embraced me until I was steady enough to be guided to his car outside.

As we drove away, I tried but couldn't bring myself to turn back for one final look at the house.

We cautiously descended the icy roads, towards town, towards London, towards her, towards telling her that though I still felt nervous about bringing a child into the world, she was the only person I'd ever want to try with. That we could figure our way through together.

'What happened?'

I looked to Mr Morrison, but no words came to me.

'Tell me everything,' he said.

'Everything?'

'From beginning to end.'

I stared at him, debating whether I should share this story what it would do to say it all out loud.

I cleared my throat, and began.

A click as the recording comes to an end.

Pause as if GEORGE is not quite sure what to do now he's finished the story.

GEORGE   Hello? Am I – I'm finished. Is it over? How do I –

The recording light switches off, and the door swings open by itself. GEORGE pauses for a moment, but then heads towards the doorway.

Hello? How do I know when it's passed on? How do I know when I'm free of it...? Hello? Anybody here?

GEORGE *exits.*

Empty room.

Pause...

    pause...

        pause.

Suddenly, from above the audience, nooses swing down all at once.

Blackout.

The End.

...after the bows, a tapping sound can be heard as the audience leaves the theatre...